Ignite Your Entrepreneurial Spark

A practical Guide to Starting and Running Your Own Business

Edward D.Rowland

Copyright

Disclaimer:

The only purpose of "Ignite Your Entrepreneurial Spark" is general information. Although Edward D. Rowland, the author, has taken great care to ensure that the material is accurate and comprehensive, it is not meant to be a source of specialized commercial, financial, legal, or professional advice. It is advised that readers consult with competent experts on their specific circumstances.

The publisher and the author disclaim all liability for any mistakes or omissions as well as for any harm brought on by using the material on this page. The reader assumes all liability for any reliance on the material in this book. Links to websites, products, or services provided by third

parties are included solely for informative reasons and do not imply endorsement. The quality or content of other resources is not the responsibility of the author.

About the author

Hey there! I'm Edward D. Rowland, the person behind "Ignite Your Entrepreneurial Spark." You know, the one who's gone through the entrepreneurial roller coaster and lived to tell the tale. I've dabbled in many businesses, learnt a ton along the way, and now I'm ready to spill the beans on what it takes to transform your aspirations into a legal business.

I'm not simply an author - I'm your virtual mentor, your cheerleader in the business game. Picture myself as that friend who's gone through the startup trenches and is now handing you the ultimate handbook. My goal? To demystify the entire "starting a business" thing and make it as real and feasible as your favorite weekend activity.

When I'm not scribbling away on my laptop, I'm out there in the real world, expressing my opinions at conferences and community events. I'm all about educating and helping small companies — it's not just about earning money; it's about producing something worthwhile.

So, dig into "Ignite Your Entrepreneurial Spark ," and let's make your company ambitions a reality. Because why only imagine it when you can achieve it, right? Cheers to your entrepreneurial adventure!

Table of content

Table of content

INTRODUCTION

Welcome to "Ignite Your Entrepreneurial Spark ," your one-stop shop for getting started on the exciting adventure of business. Whether you're a seasoned professional trying to break into the business world or a passionate individual ready to turn your ideas into reality, this book is designed to help you get there faster.

We'll tackle the basic principles of entrepreneurship in this exciting guide, integrating practical counsel with inspiring experiences from others who have traveled the entrepreneurial journey before you. Each chapter is designed to deliver concrete insights and cultivate the entrepreneurial spirit within you, from discovering your passion to developing a solid business strategy, and from recognizing market requirements to scaling up your firm.

Prepare to face obstacles, enjoy wins, and realize your full entrepreneurial potential. Ignite Your Entrepreneurial Spark is more than just a road plan; it's a partner who will help you convert your aspirations into thriving realities. Let the adventure begin!

CHAPTER 1:ENTREPRENEURIAL MINDSET

The entrepreneurial attitude is a beacon of innovation and growth in a world of perpetual change and boundless possibilities. It is not only about launching enterprises; it is also about addressing life with an inquisitive, innovative, and resourceful mindset. It's about seeing opportunities where others perceive difficulties and converting obstacles into victories.

The Essential Elements of the Entrepreneurial Mindset

•Opportunity Seeking: Entrepreneurs have an uncanny ability to see chances that others miss.

They're always looking about, asking questions, and looking for ways to better things.

•Problem-Solving: The entrepreneurial mind is hardwired to solve problems. Challenges do not frighten entrepreneurs; rather, they are viewed as puzzles to be solved. They tackle challenges creatively and analytically, looking for novel answers.

•Risk Tolerance: Successful entrepreneurs are not afraid to take measured risks. They recognize that success frequently entails moving beyond one's comfort zone and embracing the unknown.

•Resilience: The business journey is rarely easy. Setbacks, failures, and disappointments are common occurrences for entrepreneurs. They, however, do not allow these challenges define them. They instead learn from their mistakes, adapt, and endure.

•Adaptability: Because the world is always changing, entrepreneurs are masters of adaptability. They are not scared to change their strategy, adapt their goals, or accept fresh ideas.

Developing an Entrepreneurial Mindset

The entrepreneurial attitude is something you can create rather than something you are born with. Here are some tips for nurturing your inner entrepreneur:

•Embrace Curiosity: Be interested in your surroundings. Inquire, investigate fresh ideas, and challenge the current quo.

•Contest Assumptions: Don't take anything at face value. Examine assumptions, seek out opposing viewpoints, and examine alternative solutions.

•Acknowledge Failure as a Learning Experience: Failure is an unavoidable part of the business path. Don't get discouraged; instead, consider it a good learning experience.

•Seek Mentorship: Look for a mentor or an experienced entrepreneur who can advise you and give useful insights.

RECOGNIZING THE ENTREPRENEURIAL ATTITUDE

Assume you're strolling down the street and come across a damaged sidewalk. Most people would simply step over it and go about their business. An entrepreneur, on the other hand, might see the cracked sidewalk as an opportunity. "They might think,"Hey, there's a problem with this sidewalk." But I could fix it and make some money at the same time."

That sums up the entrepreneurial mindset. It's about viewing the world through new eyes, finding possibilities where others perceive hurdles, and taking action to make those opportunities a reality. Entrepreneurs are not afraid to take chances, are resourceful and resilient, and are constantly seeking fresh solutions to challenges.

Here are some fundamental characteristics of an entrepreneurial mindset:

•Seeking new possibilities: Entrepreneurs are constantly on the hunt for new prospects. They are not afraid to look outside the box and devise novel solutions to challenges.

Entrepreneurs are excellent at detecting issues and devising solutions.

•They are not afraid to take risks and attempt new things, even if they fail.
Entrepreneurs have a high risk tolerance and are prepared to take measured risks. They recognize that taking chances frequently leads to success.

•Resilience: Entrepreneurs do not give up easily. Even when things go rough, they learn from their errors and keep pushing forward.

• Flexibility: Entrepreneurs are able to change with the times. They don't hesitate to adjust their approach when necessary.

You have to develop these traits if you want to be an entrepreneur. You have to be willing to take risks and have the ability to see the world from fresh perspectives. You need to be resilient, resourceful, and flexible enough to adjust to changes.

DETERMINING YOUR ENTREPRENEURIAL FEATURES

This is a short way to identify your entrepreneurial traits:

1.Introspection

•Recall your prior encounters: Have you ever started a new project or fixed a problem on your own? Have you ever observed opportunities that others missed?

Think about your opinions and convictions: Do you think you can contribute something worthwhile and change things? Are you comfortable with risk and uncertainty?

• Assess your skills and advantages: Are you resourceful and flexible? Are you a skilled problem-solver and communicator?

2.Seek Advice from Others

•Consult your loved ones, coworkers, and friends for advice: How do people see your capacity for entrepreneurship? Do people think of you as a born leader or as a creative problem solver?

•Engage in networks and communities for entrepreneurs: Assemble a group of people who are as excited about innovation and business growth as you are.

• Consult mentors or prosperous businesspeople for guidance: Their viewpoints and thoughts may help you recognize your areas of strength and improvement.

3.Exercises in Practice

• Participate in entrepreneurial competitions or challenges: these occasions provide you the chance to test your concepts, get feedback, and get valuable experience.

•Start small businesses or side projects: Take the initiative to start small-scale ventures that will let you apply your entrepreneurial skills to practical issues.

•Donate your time and expertise: You may develop your leadership, communication, and problem-solving skills by contributing to causes that are close to your heart.

Recall that you are always learning about your entrepreneurial traits. As you gain experience, learn from your successes and failures, and hone your skills, your entrepreneurial potential will become more apparent.

FORMING A BUSINESS-FOCUSED MINDSET

The following simple actions will help you develop an entrepreneurial mindset:

•Create a growth attitude by believing that you can learn, progress, and get better. View setbacks as opportunities for improvement.

•Embrace inquiry: Show interest by looking for fresh knowledge and encounters. Ask inquiries, look into alternative perspectives, and dispel stereotypes.

•Seek for opportunities to improve procedures, address problems, or create new products or services. Think of challenges as chances to be creative.

•Take measured risks: Have an open mind and don't be afraid to step outside of your comfort zone. Make an informed decision by balancing the potential advantages with the risks.

•Learn from failures: Consider failures as teaching moments. Analyze the issue, make the necessary adjustments, and try again.

•Be flexible: Allow yourself to adjust your plans as needed. React as necessary and embrace new concepts.

•Connect with other business owners: Be in the company of individuals who are as excited about innovation and expansion as you are.

•Look for mentorship: Locate seasoned business owners who can provide insightful commentary and guidance.

• Develop your creative thinking and problem-solving skills to enhance your problem-solving abilities.

•Build collaboration and communication skills: Work with others to achieve shared objectives and effectively convey your thoughts.

Recall that developing an entrepreneurial attitude is a continuous endeavor. Your success as an entrepreneur will grow as you gain experience, grow from your successes and failures, and continue to develop your skills

CHAPTER 2: IDEA GENERATION AND VALIDATION

The two most important phases in the entrepreneurial path are idea creation and validation. Idea generation is the process of brainstorming and researching prospective business ideas, whereas validation is the process of determining the practicality and commercial potential of those ideas.

1.Concept Generation:

•Mind Mapping: Make a visual representation of your thoughts and the relationships between them.

•Brainstorming: Gather a group of individuals and urge everyone to share their ideas.

•Problem-solving: Identify common issues and create solutions that may lead to business ideas.

•Observation: Pay attention to people's actions, needs, and pain areas in order to uncover prospective possibilities.

•Research: Look at current firms, trends, and technology for ideas.

2.Validation of an Idea:

•Problem Validation: Ensure that the issue addressed by your proposal is genuine, relevant, and impacts a broad enough audience.

•Solution Validation: Confirm that your suggested solution meets the identified problem successfully.

•Market Validation: Determine if your solution is in demand and identify your target market.

•Competition Analysis: Evaluate current rivals' strengths, limitations, and market share.

•Financial Validation: Assess your idea's potential profitability and financial viability.

•Customer input: In order to measure potential consumers' interest and readiness to pay, solicit input from them.

•Prototyping: Create a prototype or minimal viable product to put your concept to the test with real users.

•Pilot Testing: Before going full-scale, conduct a small-scale pilot test to gather data and enhance your proposal.

Keep in mind that concept development and validation are iterative processes. You may need to tweak or pivot your ideas as you gain additional information and feedback.

TECHNIQUES FOR CREATING BUSINESS IDEA THROUGH BRAINSTORMING

Brainstorming is an important element in the entrepreneurial process since it is a great technique for creating innovative ideas.

Here are some easy and efficient brainstorming approaches for generating company ideas:

•Mind Mapping: Make a visual representation of your thoughts and the relationships between them. Begin with a basic concept and expand with related concepts, sub-ideas, and relationships.

•Freewriting: Without judgment or editing, write down any thought that comes to mind. Allow your thoughts to flow freely, even if they appear to be unconnected at first.

•Reverse Brainstorming: Rather than concentrating on solutions, concentrate on the issues you wish to tackle. Determine common pain areas, grievances, or unfulfilled requirements before brainstorming potential solutions.

•Brainwriting: Organize your thoughts on separate cards or sticky notes. This allows everyone to contribute anonymously and encourages quieter persons to participate.

•Role-Playing: Put yourself in the shoes of several characters, such as your ideal client, industry expert, or competition. Brainstorm ideas from their points of view.

•SCAMPER: To encourage innovation, utilize the acronym SCAMPER: Substitute, Combine, Adapt, Modify, Put to another use, Eliminate, Reverse.

•Edward de Bono's Six Thinking Hats: Use Edward de Bono's Six Thinking Hats to approach your ideas from several perspectives: White Hat (facts), Red Hat (emotions), Yellow Hat (positives), Black Hat (negatives), Green Hat (creativity), and Blue Hat (process management).

•Analogy: Get ideas from disparate disciplines or concepts. For example, how can a bird's nest affect a product design or a medical treatment have an impact on a business process?

•Collaborative Brainstorming: Bring together a group of people from various backgrounds and viewpoints to produce a broader variety of ideas. Encourage active listening and expanding on one another's thoughts.

EVALUATING THE VIABILITY OF YOUR BUSINESS CONCEPT

Before committing time, resources, and effort into developing your company concept further, you must first assess its practicality.

Here's a quick approach to determining the viability of your idea:

•Define the Problem and Solution: Clearly define the problem your concept addresses and how your suggested solution solves it effectively.

•Target Market: Identify your target clients' demographics, needs, and pain concerns. Recognize their readiness to spend as well as the size of your prospective market.

•Market Analysis: Investigate the industry landscape, identify current rivals, and evaluate their strengths, weaknesses, and market share. Examine market trends, growth prospects, and entry hurdles.

•Competitive Advantage: Determine what distinguishes your concept and how it differs from rivals. What competitive advantages will you capitalize on?

•Financial viability: Calculate your initial costs, continuing expenses, possible income sources, and profit margins. Create a financial model to forecast your future financial success.

•Operational Feasibility: Evaluate your company's operational needs, such as staffing, logistics, technology, and supply chain management.

•Legal and Regulatory Compliance: Make certain that your company complies with all applicable laws, regulations, and licensing requirements.

•input and Validation: To validate your concept and discover areas for development, solicit input from potential consumers, industry experts, and mentors.

•Risk Assessment: Determine possible risks and difficulties that your company may encounter, such as market swings, competition, technical advances, or regulatory changes. Prepare mitigating strategies.

•Adaptability and Pivot: Be ready to revise your company plan and pivot your approach if market conditions, consumer input, or new information emerge.

Remember that feasibility analysis is an iterative process. You may need to revise or pivot your concept as you gain additional information and feedback.

MARKET RESEARCH MIGHT HELP YOU VALIDATE YOUR COMPANY IDEA

Validating your company concept through market research is an important step in ensuring that your product or service has a potential market and that you are not spending time and resources on an idea that will fail.

Here are some straightforward measures you may take to confirm your company concept through market research:

•First, establish your target market. To whom are you attempting to offer your product or service? What are their needs, wants, and areas of discomfort?Once you've identified your target market, you can begin researching their habits and preferences.

•Conduct Surveys: Surveys are an excellent technique to get quantitative information about your target market. You may construct and distribute surveys using online survey tools, and you can also use surveys to gather feedback on your product or service.

•Interview Potential Customers: Interviews are an excellent technique to get qualitative information about your target market. You may conduct interviews with potential clients to discover more about their goals, needs, and problem areas. Interviews may also be used to gather feedback on your product or service.

•Analyze Industry Data:There is a wealth of industry data accessible to assist you in validating your company concept. This information may include market size, growth patterns, and competition analysis.

•Conduct Competitive Research: It is critical to understand your rivals and the services they provide to your target market. You may undertake competitive research to determine the strengths and shortcomings of your rivals, as well as potential for distinction.

•Test Your Product or Service: Testing your product or service with real clients is the greatest approach to validate your company idea. You may accomplish this by providing a free trial, running a beta test, or initiating a pilot program.

Following these steps will provide you with useful information into your target market and if your company concept has a chance of succeeding.

CHAPTER 3: CREATING A BUSINESSES PLAN

A business plan is essential for budding entrepreneurs since it acts as a road map for your company's goals, tactics, and financial predictions. A well-crafted business plan may guide your decision-making and boost your chances of success, whether you're seeking capital from investors or just want to keep on track.

1. Executive Summary:An executive summary is a succinct review of your whole business plan that highlights your company's objective, goods or services, target market, competitive advantages, financial predictions, and capital requirements. It is critical to attract the attention

of investors and present a picture of your company's potential.

2. Company Description: In the company description, go into depth about your organization's history, goal statement, ownership structure, and important staff. Explain the problem your company is attempting to solve and how your products or services address it.

3. Goods or services:Give a full explanation of your products or services, stressing their distinguishing characteristics, advantages, and target audience. Describe how your offerings vary from rivals, as well as how they meet client wants and trouble issues.

4. Market Analysis: Conduct extensive market research to comprehend the industry landscape,

which includes your target market, market size, growth trends, competition analysis, and regulatory environment. Identify potential possibilities and dangers to your business.

5. Marketing and Sales Strategy: Outline your marketing and sales strategy for reaching your target audience and meeting your sales objectives. Describe your pricing and distribution plans, promotional activities, and sales procedures.

6. Management and Organization: Introduce your management team, emphasizing their skills, expertise, and positions within the organization. Explain your organizational structure and how it contributes to your business goals.

Create thorough financial predictions, including income statements, balance sheets, and cash flow statements. Over the next three to five years, forecast your sales, costs, and profitability.

8. cash Requirements: If you're looking for cash from investors, make it clear what you need and how you intend to use the funds. Explain how the funding will help your firm grow and succeed.

9. Appendix: Include supporting papers such as important personnel resumes, market research studies, financial records, and any other relevant material that supplements your business plan in this section.

Remember that your business plan is a living document that should alter as your company develops and market conditions change. Review and update your strategy on a regular basis to verify it is still in line with your current goals and tactics.

THE VALUE OF A BUSINESS STRATEGY

A business plan is a road map for the success of your company. It defines your objectives, plans, and financial predictions, assisting you in staying on track and making sound decisions.

Here are a few of the main reasons why a business strategy is essential:

1. Clarifies your aims and objectives: Having a documented plan encourages you to describe your business's goals and objectives explicitly. This clarity will assist you in remaining focused and motivated throughout your entrepreneurial journey.

2. acts as a compass for decision-making: A business strategy acts as a compass for decision-making. It enables you to properly manage resources, prioritize activities, and make educated decisions that are consistent with your overall plan.

3. Attracts investors: A well-crafted business plan is vital if you are seeking investment from investors. It exhibits your trustworthiness, professionalism, and grasp of the potential of

your firm, enhancing your chances of obtaining money.

4. Promotes communication and cooperation: A business plan establishes a framework for communication and collaboration among team members, stakeholders, and investors. It guarantees that everyone is on the same page when it comes to the company's direction and goals.

5. Tracks progress and evaluates success: Your business plan acts as a baseline for tracking and assessing your progress and achievement. You may find areas for improvement and make necessary modifications by comparing your actual outcomes to your forecasts.

6. Improves adaptability: As market conditions shift and new possibilities emerge, a business plan enables you to adjust your plans accordingly. It offers an adaptable foundation for development and innovation.

7. Increases your chances of success: Studies show that firms with documented business plans outperform those without. A strategy boosts your chances of meeting your objectives and avoiding costly mistakes.

Recall that a company plan is an essential instrument for entrepreneurs, acting as a guide for success, attracting capital, facilitating communication, tracking advancement, and enhancing adaptability. It's an investment in the future of your business and essential to achieving your entrepreneurial objectives.

THE ELEMENT OF A THOROUGH BUSINESS PLAN

A thorough business plan serves as a roadmap for the objectives, strategies, and financial projections of your organization. It serves as a structure for choosing decisions, interacting with people, and attracting investors.

The fundamental elements of a comprehensive business strategy are as follows:

1. Executive Summary: A concise synopsis of your whole business plan that includes information on your company's goals, products or services, target market, competitive advantages, projected financials, and capital

needs. Make it engaging and educational to make a positive first impression on potential stakeholders and investors.

2. Organizational Description: In the corporate description, include information about your organization's background, mission, ownership structure, and key personnel. Describe the issue your business is trying to resolve and how your goods and services help to solve it. Stress the things that set your business apart from competitors and highlight its unique selling proposition (USP).

3. Products or offerings: Provide a thorough description of your goods or services, emphasizing their benefits, unique selling points, and intended market. Explain how your products and services differ from those of your

competitors and how they address customer needs and problems. Included should be product specifications, price strategies, and any applicable intellectual property protections.

4. Market Analysis: To fully comprehend the state of the industry, including your target market, market size, growth trends, competitive analysis, and regulatory environment, do in-depth market research. Determine the risks and opportunities that might affect your company. Look over the

Conduct a SWOT analysis of your competitive landscape, taking into account your advantages, disadvantages, opportunities, and threats.

5. Marketing and Sales Strategy: Explain how you plan to reach your target market and hit your

sales goals using marketing and sales tactics. Describe your customer relationship management (CRM) initiatives, sales procedures, promotional activities, and pricing and distribution strategy. Explain your approach to lead generation, customer acquisition, and retention for sustained business growth.

6. Management and Organization: Outline the qualifications, background, and responsibilities of your management group inside the company. Describe your organizational structure, outlining key reporting lines and decision-making processes. Present a seasoned and qualified staff that is equipped to execute the business plan.

7. Operations and Logistics: Explain your plan for manufacturing and shipping your products and services, as well as your operations strategy.

Describe your inventory management, supply chain, and fulfillment procedures. Describe the steps you've taken to improve operational efficiency and save costs while enhancing customer satisfaction.

Make detailed financial projections that include cash flow, balance sheet, and income statement information. Make a revenue, cost, and profitability prediction for the next three to five years. Provide supporting data and make reasonable assumptions to show that the project is financially feasible.

9. Cash Requirements: Clearly state your needs and your plans for using the money if you're asking investors for money. Describe how the financing will enable your company to expand and thrive. Clearly define an exit strategy for

investors, such as a purchase or initial public offering (IPO).

10. Appendix: Add any pertinent documents that support your company strategy to this area, such as financial records, market research studies, and key staff resumes. Make the appendix easy to navigate by organizing it clearly.

DEVELOPING AN INVESTOR-FRIENDLY BUSINESS PLAN

Your business plan has to tell an enticing tale that emphasizes the growth and profitability potential of your firm in order to draw in investors.

The following are some essential concepts for writing a business plan that will attract investors:

1. Emphasize a unique selling point (USP): Clearly state what makes your business unique and how it varies from competitors. Investors are drawn to novel ideas that either fulfill unfulfilled

needs or offer substantial competitive advantages.

2. Demonstrate a Large and Growing Market Opportunity: Assertively demonstrate the size and growth of the market for your products or services. Measure the market size, growth trends, and potential customer base to show that there is a need for your products or services.

3. Verify Your Target Market: Clearly identify your target customer base and show that you are cognizant of their needs, preferences, and areas of discomfort. Describe how your goods and services provide value and resolve their issues.

4. Develop an Easy-to-Understand and Profitable Business Model: Describe how your firm generates revenue and plans to turn a profit.

Investors are interested in learning about your company's capacity to make money and your strategy for expanding your market share.

5. Provide Realistic Financial Projections: Develop precise financial predictions that show your company's potential for development and profitability. Include income, balance, and cash flow statements to back up your estimates.

6. Demonstrate a Skilled and Capable Team: Highlight your management team's skills and experience, stressing their industry expertise and ability to execute the company strategy.

7. Showcase Traction and Milestones: Highlight any accomplishments you've accomplished thus far, such as customer acquisition, product

development, or collaborations. This shows momentum and boosts investor confidence.

8. Address Potential Risks and problems: Identify potential risks and problems that your company may encounter and explain how you intend to address them. Transparency and proactive risk management are valued by investors.

9. Create a Compelling Narrative: Tell your company's narrative in clear, simple, and convincing terms. Connect on an emotional level with investors and show your enthusiasm for your enterprise.

10. Tailor Your Strategy to the Correct Investors: Investigate and comprehend the individual interests and investment requirements of the

investors you intend to target. Align your business plan with their preferences and show how your organization supports their objectives.

Investors want companies with a clear path to profitability, a competent management team, and a scalable business strategy. By developing a compelling business plan that addresses these criteria, you will boost your chances of attracting investors and obtaining the capital required to realize your entrepreneurial goal.

SELECTING THE BEST BUSINESS STRUCTURE

Choosing the proper business structure is critical for any new business owner. The structure you select will have an impact on your taxes, liabilities, and capacity to obtain cash.

Here is a short approach to selecting the best business structure for your company:

1. single proprietorship: The simplest and most prevalent kind of business structure is the single proprietorship. It is owned and controlled by a single individual who is personally accountable for all of the company's debts and liabilities.

2. A partnership is a firm that is owned and run by two or more persons. Partners share in the company's revenues and losses, and they are individually accountable for any debts and responsibilities.

3. Limited Liability Company (LLC): A limited liability company (LLC) is a hybrid business

form that combines the characteristics of a corporation and a partnership. LLCs provide their owners with limited liability protection, which means that their personal assets are normally protected from corporate debts and liabilities.

4. Corporation: A corporation is a legal entity distinct from its owners. This implies that the corporation is liable for its own debts and obligations, and the corporation's owners are not personally liable for the corporation's debts.

Consider the following factors while selecting a business structure:

•culpability: How much personal culpability are you willing to accept? If personal responsibility is a concern, an LLC or corporation may be a better option than a sole proprietorship or partnership.

•Taxes: In general, sole proprietorships and partnerships are taxed as "pass-through" businesses, which means that business revenue is passed through to the owners' personal tax returns. LLCs can be taxed as either a pass-through business or as a corporation. Corporations are taxed separately from individuals.

•Formations: Sole proprietorships and partnerships are simple to set up and run. Although LLCs need additional paperwork and formality, they are not as complicated as corporations. Corporations are the most difficult corporate structure to establish and run.

•Raising cash: A corporation may be a better alternative than an LLC or partnership if you need to raise capital from investors. This is due to the fact that firms may issue stock, which can then be sold to investors.

Finally, consulting with an attorney and a tax expert is the best approach to determine the correct business structure for your company. They can assist you in understanding the benefits and drawbacks of each structure and making the best selection for your specific scenario.

CHAPTER 4:LEGAL AND FINANCIAL CONSIDERATIONS

Considerations for Legal

When beginning a firm, it is critical to understand the legal requirements and repercussions.

The following are some important legal issues for businesses:

•Business Structure: Select an appropriate business structure, such as a sole proprietorship, partnership, limited liability company (LLC), or corporation. Each structure has distinct legal and tax consequences.

•Business Licenses and Permits: Obtain the appropriate local, state, and federal business licenses and permits. The particular licenses and permissions needed will depend on the sort of business you run.

•Tax Registration: Register with the proper tax authorities, such as the Internal Revenue Service and your state tax agency. If you intend to hire staff, you must get an Employer Identification Number (EIN).

•Protection of Intellectual Property: Protect your intellectual property, such as trademarks, copyrights, and patents. It may be necessary to register your trademarks and copyrights with the United States Patent and Trademark Office.

•Contracts: Review and sign written contracts with workers, suppliers, customers, and other company partners. Contracts should explicitly define each agreement's terms and circumstances.

•Law and Regulation Compliance: Comply with all relevant rules and regulations, including labor laws, environmental laws, and consumer protection laws.

Considerations for Finance

Financial planning is essential for every business's success.

The following are some important financial concerns for businesses:

•Business Plan: Create a detailed business plan outlining your financial objectives, strategies, and predictions. This will allow you to keep track of your progress and make more educated financial decisions.

•Financial Statements: Prepare financial statements such as income statements, balance sheets, and cash flow statements on a regular basis. These statements will provide you a glimpse of your company's financial condition.

•Budgeting and Forecasting: Make a budget and forecast your revenue and spending on a regular basis. This will assist you in managing your cash flow and ensuring that you are on track to reach your financial objectives.

•Accounting and Tax Planning: Seek expert accounting and tax planning assistance to maintain compliance and optimize earnings.

•Funding sources: If you need more funds to build your business, look into various funding sources such as loans, grants, or investments.

•Identify and analyze possible financial risks such as market fluctuations, competition, and regulatory changes. Implement risk-mitigation methods.

Keep in mind that legal and financial concerns are a constant component of running a successful business. Maintain current knowledge of important rules and regulations, handle your funds properly, and seek expert help when necessary.

SELECTING THE BEST BUSINESS STRUCTURE

One of the most important decisions you'll make when beginning a business is deciding on the correct business structure. The structure you choose will have an effect on your taxes, liabilities, and capacity to obtain money.

Let's have a look at some of the most frequent business formats and their essential considerations:

1 proprietorship sole:

Pros: Easy to set up and run, no business taxes
Cons: Unlimited personal responsibility, restricted capital access

2.Partnership:

Benefits include shared resources and knowledge, as well as flexible profit sharing.

Cons: All partners have unlimited personal liability, and the legal framework is complicated.

3.LLC (Limited Liability Company):

Advantages: Limited liability protection and the option of pass-through taxation

Cons: There is more paperwork and procedures involved than with a sole proprietorship or partnership.

4.Corporation:

Advantages: Limited liability protection, the opportunity to issue shares, and a distinct legal organization.

Cons: Most difficult to design and run business structure, double taxes.

CONSIDERATIONS FOR THE BEST BUSINESS STRUCTURE

•Personal Liability: What level of personal risk are you ready to accept? An LLC or corporation may be preferable if you wish to safeguard your personal assets from company obligations.

•Taxes: Partnerships and sole proprietorships are normally taxed as "pass-through" businesses, whereas corporations are taxed separately. Think about the tax consequences.

•Business Activities: Athen LLC or corporation can protect your personal assets if your business involves high-risk activities.

•Growth Plans: If you want to raise funds or develop rapidly, the capacity of a corporation to issue shares might be useful.

•Complexity: Sole proprietorships and partnerships are easier to administer, but LLCs and corporations need more paperwork.

Choosing the correct business structure is a critical step in preparing your company for success. To make the best option for your unique case, carefully consider these aspects and contact an attorney or tax professional.

RECOGNIZING THE LEGAL PREREQUISITES FOR LAUNCHING A BUSINESS

Understanding the fundamentals of the legal requirements for launching a business will help you traverse the process efficiently.

Here's a quick rundown of the essential legal criteria for launching a business:

1. Select a Business Structure: Select the best business structure for your needs, such as a sole proprietorship, partnership, LLC, or corporation. Each structure has its own set of legal and tax consequences.

2. Register Your Company Name: Register your company name with the relevant municipal or state government office. This helps to create your company's identification and prevents your name from being used by others.

3. Obtain Business Licenses and permissions: Depending on your business's activity and location, you may require special licenses and permissions from local, state, or federal authorities. Zoning permissions, health permits, and environmental permits are examples of these.

4. Register for Tax Identification Numbers: If you want to hire staff or open a company bank account, obtain an Employer Identification Number (EIN) from the IRS. Register for sales

and use taxes with the relevant state tax department.

5. Obey Labor Laws: Obey all relevant labor laws, including minimum wage standards, overtime pay rules, and anti-discrimination statutes.

6. Protect Intellectual Property: To protect your intellectual property rights, consider registering your unique creations, such as logos, trademarks, or innovations, with the United States Patent and Trademark Office (USPTO).

7. Obtain Insurance:Secure suitable insurance, such as general liability insurance, property insurance, and workers' compensation insurance, to protect your firm from potential dangers.

8. Seek Legal and Professional Advice: Speak with an attorney and a tax expert to verify you are following all legal requirements and making educated decisions about your business structure, taxes, and contracts.

Remember that legal requirements may differ based on the type of business, region, and operational activities. Staying knowledgeable about local legislation and getting expert advice as needed will assist you in efficiently navigating the legal landscape

MANAGING FINANCE AND SECURING FUNDING

Effective financial management and funding are critical components of running a successful business.

Here's a quick tutorial to help you traverse these critical areas:

•Establish Financial Systems: Implement dependable accounting and bookkeeping systems to track your revenue, spending, assets, and obligations. This will provide you a comprehensive view of your financial situation.

•Create a Budget: Create a thorough budget outlining your predicted revenue and spending for a specified time period. To keep on track, examine and alter your budget on a regular basis.

•Manage Cash Flow: Keep a tight eye on your cash flow to ensure you have the finances to satisfy your ongoing obligations. To predict possible financial shortages, use cash flow forecasting tools.

•Monitor Expenses: Implement expenditure management strategies to reduce wasteful spending. Regularly review spending and find areas for potential cost reductions.

•Keep correct and Organized Financial Records: Maintain correct and organized financial records, including invoices, receipts, and tax paperwork. These data will be required for tax purposes and financial analysis.

Obtaining Funding:

•Assess financing Requirements: Determine the precise amount of financing necessary for your company's objectives, such as expansion, new product development, or marketing campaigns.

•Explore Funding sources: Investigate various funding sources for businesses, such as loans, grants, crowdsourcing, and venture capital. Each option has its own set of conditions, qualifying requirements, and applicability for different phases of operation.

•Write a complete Business Plan: Write a complete business plan that contains your business concept, financial estimates, and market analysis. This will be an important document when looking for money from investors or lenders.

Attend industry events, join entrepreneurial networks, and network with possible investors or financing sources. Building contacts and demonstrating your company's potential can lead to financial opportunities.

•Seek Professional Help: Speak with professional financial advisers or business consultants to help you navigate the funding procedure. They can assist you in identifying the best funding choices and preparing the relevant documentation.

Keep in mind that financial management and financing acquisition are continual activities that need constant attention and change. Staying up to date on financial legislation, seeking new financing sources, and modifying your financial plans as your firm expands will all help you achieve long-term financial success.

CHAPTER 5: MARKETING AND SALES STRATEGIES

Marketing Strategies:

Identify Your Target Audience: Find out who your ideal clients are by researching their needs, preferences, and areas of discomfort. This will enable you to effectively modify your marketing strategies and messaging.

• Establish Marketing Objectives: Specify and measure your marketing goals, such as increasing revenue, lead generation, or brand awareness. Your marketing efforts will be guided by these goals, which also let you gauge their success.

Establish a unique selling proposition (USP): Describe what sets your business apart from the competition and what makes it unique. Your target audience should find your unique selling proposition (USP) appealing, and it should highlight your competitive advantages.

•Produce Interesting Content: Write excellent content that is interesting, instructive, and pertinent to your intended audience. Distribute your content on a variety of channels, such as your website, email marketing, and social media.

•Make the Most of Social Media Platforms: Connect with your target market, build relationships, and advertise your company on social media. To draw in more followers, interact with them, respond to their comments, and run relevant ads.

•Optimize Your Website: Ensure that your website is optimized for search engines, visually appealing, and easy to use. Make it simple for people to contact you, give clear information about your goods or services, and use relevant keywords in order to attract organic traffic.

Sales Strategies:

Establish a Sales Process: Clearly define the steps involved in finding, evaluating, and turning leads into paying customers. It is imperative that this process be repeatable and consistent in order to ensure successful sales cycles.

•Build genuine Relationships with Prospective Customers: Give your whole attention to getting to know potential customers, learning about their issues, and offering customized solutions. Utilize a range of communication channels to nurture leads, such as email, phone calls, and in-person meetings.

• Explain Your Proposition for Value In effect: Clearly state the benefits your business offers prospective customers. Stress how your offerings fulfill their wants, resolve their problems, and improve their quality of life.

• Handle Objections Effectively: Prepare well-rehearsed responses to likely objections from customers. Show empathy, deal with problems right away, and offer other options when necessary.

•Negotiate Effectively: Be ready to haggle with customers to create circumstances that will benefit both parties. To reach your sales goals, research market rates, comprehend your profit margins, and be willing to make concessions.

•Track and Measure Sales Performance: Monitor your sales performance information, such as revenue, volume, and conversion rates. After identifying opportunities for development through data analysis, optimize your sales strategies.

Keep in mind that sales and marketing are complementary and closely related activities. great marketing draws in and develops prospects, and great sales strategies turn those leads into paying customers. By using these easy strategies, your business may increase sales, generate leads, and improve brand recognition.

CHOOSING YOUR POSSIBLE MARKET

Establishing your target market is a crucial first step in developing a successful marketing and sales plan for your business. It is necessary to know the exact demographic that you hope to attract with your goods or services. By correctly defining your target market, you can adapt your messaging, channels, and overall approach to their needs and preferences.

Take into account the following factors when identifying your target market:

•Demographics: Find out the age, gender, location, income, education, and lifestyle characteristics of your prospective clientele. This information will help you understand their background and tastes.

• Psychographics: Look at the psychological factors influencing your target audience's actions and choices. Consider their objectives, values, attitudes, and areas of interest.

•Requirements and Pain Points: Determine the exact problems, challenges, or unfulfilled needs that your products or services address. Comprehending their areas of discomfort will enable you to appropriately arrange your offerings.

• Online Behavior: Look at the websites, social media accounts, and search habits of your target market as well as how they use the internet. This will function as a guide for your online marketing endeavors.

• Purchase Habits: Find out where and how your target market shops, as well as the factors that influence their decisions. This will help you choose the most effective sales channels and messaging.

After you have gathered data about your target market, you may create a comprehensive profile of your perfect customer. The person you are trying to get in touch with should have their needs, habits, psychographics, and demographics included in this profile.

Here are some additional guidelines to help you identify your target market:

•Analyze market trends, survey prospective customers, compile secondary data, and conduct market research.

• Examine your present clientele to see who is already interested in your offers. Find out what characteristics your current clients have in common.

• Request feedback from the sales and customer service team: Obtain data from employees who interact directly with customers.

• Monitor online discussions and critiques: To gain a better understanding of others' tastes and concerns, pay attention to what they have to say about your industry and the competitors.

If you take the time and make the effort to identify your target market, you may create targeted marketing campaigns, provide pertinent goods or services, and eventually accomplish your business objectives more successfully.

DEVELOPMENT OF EFFECTIVE MARKETING STRATEGIES

Businesses of all sizes need to design effective marketing strategies in order to reach their target audience, generate leads, and drive sales.

Here's a short guide on developing and putting into action successful marketing campaigns:

1. Clearly State Your Marketing Goals: Whether it's increasing brand awareness, generating leads, or boosting sales, make sure your marketing goals are clear.

Establish SMART (specific, measurable, achievable, relevant, and time-bound) objectives so that you can monitor your development and evaluate the impact of your campaigns.

2. Know Your Target Audience: Determine who your ideal customers are by looking at their wants, pain points, psychographics, and demographics.

Create buyer personas to reflect distinct parts of your target audience, enabling you to successfully adjust your messaging and strategy.

3.Create an Appealing Value Proposition: Explain the distinct value your company provides to your target audience.

Emphasize how your products or services solve their issues, meet their needs, and make their lives better.

4.Select the Best Marketing Channels: Determine the channels your target audience uses, such as social networking platforms, search engines, or email.

Choose an online and offline channel mix that fits your budget, target audience, and marketing objectives.

Create high-quality content that is useful, relevant, and resonates with your target audience.

Use a variety of content types, such as blog entries, infographics, videos, and social media postings.

5.Search Engine Optimization:Utilize search engine optimization (SEO) tactics to guarantee your website ranks high in search engine results pages (SERPs).

Use relevant keywords, improve page titles and meta descriptions, and establish backlinks from credible websites.

6.Create Efficient Email Marketing Campaigns:Collect potential clients' email addresses and segment your email list depending on their interests or habits.

Create targeted email campaigns with eye-catching subject lines, interesting content, and clear calls to action.

7.Utilize Social Media Platforms: Create engaging social media profiles and provide relevant material that resonates with your target audience on a regular basis.

To reach a larger audience, interact with followers, reply to comments, and run targeted advertisements.

8.Track and Analyze Your Results: Use analytics tools to analyze the effectiveness of your marketing activities and determine what works and what needs to be improved.

Continuously update your data-driven strategy to respond to shifting market conditions or audience preferences.

9.Seek Professional Advice: If you need help designing, launching, or managing your marketing initiatives, consider speaking with marketing specialists or agencies.

Their experience may assist you in optimizing your strategy, maximizing your money, and efficiently achieving your marketing objectives.

Remember that good marketing is a continual process that needs constant modification and refining. You can establish customized marketing campaigns, attract your ideal clients, and drive business success by following these simple tactics.

ESTABLISHING A STRONG PIPELINE

Building a robust sales pipeline is critical for organizations of all sizes to create leads, nurture them through the sales process, and complete agreements on a continuous basis. A healthy sales pipeline assures a consistent flow of potential clients, enhancing your chances of meeting sales targets and driving business development.

Here's a quick method to creating a robust sales pipeline:

1. Establish your ideal client profile (ICP):

•Determine your ideal consumers' unique qualities, such as demographics, industry, pain areas, and purchase habits.

•Knowing your ICP allows you to focus your sales efforts on the best qualified prospects and boost your conversion rate.

2.Develop a clear sales process:

•Define the various stages of your sales process, from early lead generation to contract closure.

•Develop a consistent procedure that explains the activities involved in each stage, as well as the actions that salespeople should follow.

•Having a well-defined sales process assures consistency, boosts efficiency, and raises the probability of closing business.

3.Put in place efficient prospecting strategies:

•Find high-quality lead sources, such as industry events, internet directories, or social media platforms.

•Utilize appropriate keywords and search engine optimization (SEO) tactics to drive traffic to your website.

•Generate leads by using targeted web advertising to reach particular parts of your audience.

4. Effectively qualify leads:

•Create a qualifying procedure to determine whether prospective clients meet your ICP and are really interested in your products or services.

•Assess their requirements, budget, and decision-making power to guarantee a suitable fit for your offers.

•Prioritize qualified leads that match your desired client profile and are more likely to close.

5.Generate leads using the sales funnel:

•Create individualized nurturing efforts based on each lead's interests and requirements.

•To educate leads and demonstrate your expertise, provide helpful information such as blog articles, whitepapers, or case studies.

•Build relationships with leads via email, phone conversations, or social media to keep your brand top-of-mind.

6.Continuous follow-up:

•Develop a regular follow-up cycle to avoid potential consumers falling through the cracks.

•Use a customer relationship management (CRM) system to track conversations, schedule follow-ups, and track the progress of leads.

•Adjust your follow-up strategy based on the lead's degree of involvement and interest in your products.

7.Effectively close deals:

•Give your sales staff the skills and training they need to complete deals successfully.

•Offer explicit counsel on contract negotiations, resolving objections, and overcoming buying hurdles.

•Encourage sales and marketing teams to work together to enable a smooth transition from lead creation to completing agreements.

8.Refine and analyze your sales process:

•Review your sales pipeline data on a regular basis to discover areas for improvement and evaluate your progress toward targets.

•Analyze conversion rates, average deal size, and sales cycle time to discover sales process strengths and shortcomings.

•Make data-driven changes to your strategy, approaches, and message to improve your sales funnel and outcomes.

Remember that developing a great sales funnel is a continual activity that needs constant work and modification. By applying these simple tactics, you may acquire quality leads, cultivate their interest, and convert them into paying clients, therefore fueling your company's development and success.

CHAPTER 6: MANAGEMENT AND TEAM BUILDING

A joyful and productive work environment as well as the achievement of business goals depend on effective team formation and management. Here's a brief manual on creating, managing, and keeping a successful team:

Putting a Group Together:

1. Identify the team's roles and responsibilities:

• Clearly outline the duties and responsibilities of every team member so that everyone is aware of their contributions and expectations.

•Assign duties and projects based on individual capabilities, abilities, and experience to improve team efficiency.

2. Identify the Correct Persons:

•Assign candidates who fulfill the needs and objectives of your team by having the necessary skills, background, and cultural fit.

•To make sure you recruit the right individuals, do in-depth interviews, evaluate behavioral talents, and gauge cultural fit.

3..Efficiently Acclimate New Workers:

• Provide a comprehensive onboarding process that acquaints new hires with the work environment, team dynamics, and their specific role.

•Assign pals or mentors to help new team members get settled in and offer support throughout their first few weeks.

Leading a Team:

1. Establish Open Lines of Communication

•To foster honest and open communication, organize frequent brainstorming meetings, problem-solving sessions, and feedback sessions.

•Make use of platforms and communication techniques that encourage information sharing and teamwork.

2. Establish reasonable expectations and goals:

Collaborate with your group to establish measurable, attainable targets that align with the overall business goals.

• Break large goals down into smaller benchmarks in order to track development, recognize success, and maintain motivation.

3. Encourage and Have Faith in Your Group:

Assign team members the freedom and authority to make decisions within the parameters of their duties. Encourage initiative and creativity by praising and rewarding both individual and group accomplishments.

4. Consistently offer coaching and feedback:

• Consistently provide team members positive feedback, emphasizing their strengths as well as areas for improvement.

•Offer coaching and mentoring to help people grow as people, get over challenges, and realize their full potential.

5. Take initiative to resolve disputes and problems:

•Establish a safe and encouraging environment where team members may voice concerns or differences.

•Mediate conflicts and assist in settlement; resolve issues impartially and promptly.

6.Acknowledge and appreciate successes:

•Build a culture of gratitude and acknowledgment by recognizing and respecting both individual and group contributions.

•To boost spirits, drive, and involvement, celebrate successes, landmarks, and victories.

7. Promote Development and Lifelong Learning:

•Support and encourage team members as they look for chances to continue learning and developing.

•Offer staff mentorship, workshops, or training to help them develop their skills, stay up to date on industry developments, and foster personal development.

Keep in mind that building and leading a team requires commitment, flexibility, and a commitment to fostering a positive and productive work environment. By using these easy strategies, you can inspire your staff to do great things and add to the success of your company.

SELECTING THE CORRECT TALENT

Specify what you need:

1. Determine the role that needs to be filled: Make sure you understand the exact position you need to be in, including its responsibilities, requirements, and level of expertise.

2. Evaluate your company's beliefs and culture to make sure the applicant will fit in with the team and the business.

3. Consider your budget: Determine the range of pay and benefits you can provide to draw in and keep excellent employees.

Make a compelling job description.

1. Use clear, basic language: Write a job description that is easy to understand and devoid of technical terms.

2. elucidate the primary duties: Clearly state the fundamental responsibilities and requirements of the position.

3. Describe the minimal training and work history required for the position.

4.Include the relevant competencies: List the abilities, know-how, and skills needed for the position

.

5. Describe the benefits and privileges you provide, such as paid time off, health insurance, and a variety of compensation.

Potential references:

1.Post job opening notices on appropriate business websites, social media platforms, and online job boards

.

2. Attend industry events: To network with potential clients, go to business conferences, trade shows, and professional gatherings.

3.Make use of employee referrals: Encourage current workers to suggest eligible prospects from their network.

4.Reach out to passive candidates: Identify and contact talented individuals who are not actively seeking for new opportunities but may be interested in yours.

Examine resumes and cover letters:

1.credentials review: Determine if the candidate's credentials and experience match the job criteria.

2.Evaluate skills and competencies: Examine the candidate's résumé for evidence of the needed skills, knowledge, and abilities.

3.Evaluate cultural fit: Determine whether the candidate's values and personality are compatible with the corporate culture.

Perform phone screenings:

1.Ask about their interest in the role: Determine the amount of interest the candidate has in the position and the firm.

2.Talk about their experience and qualifications: Inquire about their relevant job experience, abilities, and accomplishments.

3. Evaluate their communication abilities: Assess the candidate's ability to speak clearly and effectively.

Organize interviews for eligible candidates:

1.Conduct structured interviews: Use a structured interview approach in which all candidates are asked the same questions.

2.Assess technical skills: Assess the candidate's technical abilities and knowledge as they relate to the position.

3.Evaluate problem-solving abilities: Present hypothetical scenarios to the candidate and analyze their problem-solving strategy.

4.Determine cultural fit: Inquire about the candidate's values, demeanor, and work style.

Make an offer and get started:

1.Negotiate the pay and benefits: Talk with the chosen applicant about the compensation, benefits, and start date.

2.Send a formal offer letter: Make a written offer letter explaining the conditions of employment available to the candidate.

3.Introduce the new recruit to the corporate culture, team dynamics, and their unique function through a thorough onboarding process.

CREATING A POSITIVE AND PRODUCTIVE WORKPLACE

1. Be a positive role model.

•Be cheerful, upbeat, and supportive in the workplace to set a good tone.

•Express gratitude for your workers' hard work and devotion.

•Be personable and willing to listen to comments.

2. Encourage interaction.

•Create a climate in which employees feel free to express their thoughts and concerns.

•Hold frequent team meetings and one-on-one sessions with staff to check in.

•Utilize communication technologies to keep in touch with your colleagues even if you are not in the same workplace.

3. Encourage collaboration.

•Inspire staff to work together on projects.

•Organize team-building activities such as social gatherings or volunteer initiatives.

•Recognize and reward collaboration.

4. Create a learning and development culture.

•Encourage staff to participate in training courses and industry events.

•Make chances for workers to mentor one another available.

•Construct a knowledge-sharing platform where staff may discuss best practices and tips.

5. Be adaptable.

•Provide flexible work options, such as telecommuting or flextime.

•Be empathetic if employees need to take personal time off.

•Be adaptable to changing conditions.

You can establish a happy and productive work atmosphere that attracts and retains top talent by following these easy recommendations.

EFFECTIVE TASKS DELEGATION

Managers must delegate work efficiently in order to maximize their time, empower their team members, and guarantee projects are finished successfully.

Here's a quick method to efficiently distributing tasks:

1.Select the best individual for the job: When allocating duties, consider each team member's talents, weaknesses, and availability. To enhance productivity and engagement, assign activities that match their talents and interests.

2.Define the task clearly: Provide clear and succinct task instructions, including objectives, deliverables, timeframes, and any relevant restrictions or limits. Make sure there is no confusion regarding what has to be done.

3.Empower your team members: Give team members adequate authority and autonomy to make decisions and take responsibility for their given duties. Delegate responsibility for the job as well as the work itself.

4.Set expectations and check-in points: Establish clear expectations for the quality of work as well as completion timeframes. Schedule frequent check-ins to track progress, give assistance, and resolve any issues that arise.

5.Provide continuing help and feedback: As your team members work on their assigned responsibilities, provide ongoing assistance and feedback. Make yourself accessible to answer questions, give advice, and provide constructive comments to help them develop their abilities.

6.Recognize and appreciate: Recognize and appreciate your team members' efforts and successes when they successfully fulfill allotted responsibilities. Recognize their efforts and encourage good conduct.

7.Reflect on the process and suggest opportunities for improvement. To improve your delegation abilities over time, evaluate your work selection, communication strategies, and check-in frequency.

Remember that effective delegation requires a delicate balance of offering clear instructions while also allowing your team members to take responsibility for their job. You can empower your team to flourish, enhance productivity, and achieve organizational goals more effectively by following these simple tactics.

CHAPTER 7 :OPERATION AND LOGISTICS

Operations

The procedures and actions that convert inputs into outputs are referred to as operations. In the context of business, operations refer to the complete process of developing and providing goods or services to clients. Production, inventory management, order fulfillment, and customer service are examples of such jobs.

Logistics

The planning and execution of the transfer of products and information from origin to destination is referred to as logistics.

Transportation, warehousing, and distribution are examples of such jobs.

Operations and logistics play an important part in a company.
Operations and logistics are vital to the success of any company. They assist enterprises in the following ways:

•cut expenses: Businesses may cut manufacturing, transportation, and inventory management costs by streamlining operations and logistics procedures.

•Improve efficiency: Businesses may increase their efficiency and productivity by optimizing their operations and logistical procedures.

•boost customer satisfaction: Businesses may boost customer satisfaction by offering exceptional customer service and delivering items or services on schedule and in full.

Case studies in operations and logistics

Here are some instances of how operations and logistics are applied in various industries:

•Operations are used by a manufacturing organization to convert raw resources into completed goods. The final items are subsequently transported to merchants or customers via logistics.

•A retail firm manages inventory levels and product movement via operations. After that, logistics is utilized to deliver items from distribution facilities to retail locations.

•Operations are used by a service firm to manage client service requests and send service professionals. After that, logistics is utilized to plan and route service professionals to client locations.

Operations and logistics are critical to the success of any company that manufactures or distributes goods or services. Businesses may save costs, enhance productivity, and raise customer happiness by understanding and improving these processes.

ESTABLISHING EFFECTIVE OPERATIONAL PROCESSES

It is critical for organizations of all sizes to have effective operational procedures in order to streamline their activities, increase production, and fulfill organizational goals.

Here's a quick approach on establishing effective operating processes:

1.Identify and document existing processes:

•Begin by meticulously sketching out your present operating procedures, including the tasks involved, the resources needed, and the persons in charge.

•Use flowcharts, diagrams, or extensive explanations to fully document each step to ensure a clear grasp of the existing workflow.

2.Identify and Analyze Inefficiencies:

•Examine each process critically, discovering areas of duplication, bottlenecks, or superfluous procedures that impede efficiency.

•To identify opportunities for improvement, analyze the time spent on each activity, the resources used, and the overall flow of the process.

3.Develop Specific Process Goals:

•For each operational process, establish precise, measurable, attainable, relevant, and time-bound (SMART) goals.

•Develop specific targets that connect with the overarching business goals and solve identified inefficiencies.

4. Simplify and standardize processes:

•Redesign processes to remove superfluous stages, consolidate repeated operations, and automate repetitive actions as much as feasible.

•In order to assure consistency, eliminate variability, and minimize mistakes, standardize procedures across the business.

5.Incorporate Technology and Automation:

•Utilize technology to automate regular operations, simplify data gathering and analysis, and improve communication and cooperation.

•To simplify processes, investigate software options, process automation tools, and project management platforms.

6.Employee Empowerment and Engagement:

•Involve employees in the process improvement program by soliciting their opinions, ideas, and expertise.

•Encourage staff to take responsibility for their jobs, give them the appropriate training, and detect and recommend changes.

7.Continuously monitor and improve:

•Develop key performance indicators (KPIs) to assess the efficacy of the revised procedures.

•Monitor process performance on a regular basis, identify areas for improvement, and make modifications as appropriate.

•Promote a continuous improvement culture by encouraging staff to find and offer process improvements.

Remember that establishing effective operational procedures is a constant journey that needs regular review, modification, and improvement. You may simplify your processes, increase efficiency, and achieve organizational success by using these simple tactics.

INVENTORY AND SUPPLY CHAIN MANAGEMENT

Inventory and supply chain management are critical for organizations of all sizes to assure product availability, reduce costs, and retain a competitive advantage. Here's a quick primer on inventory and supply chain management:

Inventory Control:

1. Establish Inventory Levels:

•Determine ideal inventory levels by analyzing past sales data, seasonal trends, and client demand patterns.

•Establish safety stock levels to protect against unforeseen variations in demand or supply interruptions.

2. Establish Inventory Control Systems:

•Use inventory management software or create manual processes to keep track of inventory levels, reorder points, and stock movements.

•Conduct inventory audits on a regular basis to reconcile physical inventory with recorded numbers and discover inconsistencies.

3. Reduce Inventory Costs:

•To decrease procurement costs, negotiate favorable terms with suppliers, examine price choices, and investigate bulk discounts.

•Utilize just-in-time (JIT) inventory management solutions to reduce carrying expenses and storage needs.

Logistics Management:

1. Identify Important Supply Chain Partners:

•Select trustworthy and cost-effective suppliers, taking into account quality, delivery performance, and ethical standards.

•Build good connections with suppliers by encouraging open communication and problem-solving collaboration.

2. Simplify Supply Chain Operations:

•To increase logistics efficiency, optimize transportation routes, use consolidation tactics, and leverage technology.

•Use supply chain visibility technologies to follow products in transit, check inventory levels, and foresee any delays.

3. Manage Risks in the Supply Chain:

•Recognize possible risks such as natural catastrophes, economic changes, and supply interruptions.

•Develop risk-mitigation strategies, such as diversifying suppliers, stockpiling safety supplies, and developing alternate transportation routes.

4.Accept Supply Chain Technology:

•Utilize supply chain management (SCM) tools to improve inventory levels and streamline procedures.

•Utilize data analytics to get insights into supply chain performance, find opportunities for improvement, and make educated decisions.

A holistic approach to inventory and supply chain management is required for effective inventory and supply chain management, which balances product availability, cost efficiency, and risk mitigation. Businesses may simplify their processes, improve customer happiness, and achieve long-term success by using these basic tactics.

CUSTOMER ORDER COMPLETION AND EXCELLENT CUSTOMER SERVICE

Customer orders must be filled and exceptional customer service must be provided in order for businesses of all sizes to retain consumers, generate repeat business, and develop a favorable reputation.

Here's a general lesson on how to get started:

Order Processing:

1. Simplify Order Processing:

•Install an effective order management system to track orders from start to finish.

•Automate order processing procedures including payment processing, inventory allocation, and shipping label creation.

2. Ensure Order Picking and Packing Accuracy:

•Use barcode scanning or RFID technology to reduce picking mistakes and assure correct fulfillment.

•Use qualified and experienced warehouse staff to handle product packaging and assure damage-free delivery.

3. Rush Order Shipping:

•Partner with dependable and cost-effective shipping providers to ensure order delivery on time.

•Provide a variety of shipping choices to satisfy consumer preferences and delivery deadlines.

4. Supply Order Tracking and Notifications:

•Provide real-time order tracking to clients via web portals or email notifications.

•Respond to customer inquiries about order status, shipment progress, and projected delivery dates on a frequent basis.

Customer Support:

1. Clearly define customer service policies:

•Develop explicit policies and processes for customer service interactions, including as response times, resolution methods, and escalation protocols.

•Train customer service staff to address questions in a professional, compassionate, and efficient manner.

2. Provide a variety of customer service channels:

•Make it easy for consumers to contact your support service by phone, email, live chat, and social media.
•Install a ticketing system to track and prioritize client inquiries, allowing for quick resolutions.

3. Actively Listen and Respond to Concerns:
•Listen actively to client issues, sympathize with their situations, and show real concern.

•Explain things clearly and concisely, give solutions to problems, and apologize for any difficulties.

4. Go Above and Beyond:

•Outperform client expectations by going above and beyond to address problems and give great service.

•Provide individual help, proactive support, and a dedication to client satisfaction.

5. Constantly strive to improve customer service:

•Use surveys, reviews, and direct encounters to seek feedback from consumers on a regular basis.

•Analyze customer input to find areas for improvement, make changes, and improve customer service delivery on a continuing basis.

Remember that completing client orders and delivering exceptional customer service is a continuous process that involves devotion, empathy, and a dedication to customer happiness. By using these straightforward tactics, you may increase customer loyalty, improve brand reputation, and create long-term economic success.

CHAPTER 8: EXPANSION AND GROWTH

In business, expansion and growth are closely connected ideas. Growth is the process of raising a business's value or profitability, whereas expansion is the act of growing a business's size or scope. For companies of all sizes, growth and expansion are crucial because they may raise sales, market share, and brand recognition.

There are several approaches to corporate growth and expansion. Several popular tactics consist of:

• Entering new markets: This might entail setting up shop somewhere, concentrating on a different clientele, or branching out into uncharted territory.

•producing new goods or services: This might entail adding new features or benefits to the present lineup, expanding the product line, or producing whole new goods or services that have nothing to do with what's already available.

• Purchasing other companies or combining with them can be a fast method to grow and have access to new markets, resources, and skills.

•Increasing operational efficiency might entail cutting expenses, simplifying procedures, or making new technology investments.

•Improving lead generation, transaction closure, and brand recognition are some examples of how to improve marketing and sales activities.

The ideal development and expansion plan will differ based on the particular firm and its objectives. Nonetheless, there are a few broad guidelines that might support companies in their attempts to develop and expand. Among these guidelines are:

•Having a clear strategy: Companies looking to expand and grow should have a clear plan in place. Timelines, targets, and precise goals should all be part of this strategy.

• Being adaptive and flexible: Since the business environment is ever-changing, companies must be both in their attempts to develop and expand. This entails having the flexibility to adjust their plans as necessary.

• Investing in people and resources: In order to support their development and growth initiatives, businesses must invest in the people and resources they require. This entails acquiring sufficient funding, investing in new technology, and employing competent workers.

• Monitoring results and making adjustments: Companies should keep an eye on their development and growth goals, adjusting them as necessary. This will enable them to stay on course and accomplish their objectives.

While development and expansion can be difficult, they are necessary for companies of all sizes to be competitive and prosper over the long run. Businesses may improve their chances of success in their development and expansion initiatives by adhering to the aforementioned guidelines.

IDENTIFYING GROWTH OPPORTUNITIES

Identifying growth possibilities is critical for organizations of all sizes to stay competitive and achieve long-term success.

Here's a quick method to recognizing chances for growth:

1. Examine your present operations:

•Determine your key capabilities, competitive advantages, and opportunities for improvement.

•Analyze your market share, client base, and competition landscape.

•Analyze your financial performance: Examine your sales, earnings, and costs to discover opportunities for improvement.

2. Conduct market research:

•Understand the requirements and desires of your customers: Conduct market research to uncover customer trends, unmet needs, and pain spots.

•Track industry trends and changes to identify potential opportunities and dangers.

•Monitor your competition: Identify and assess your significant competitors' strategy, strengths, and shortcomings.

3. Consider prospective areas for expansion:

•Compare your present business, target market, and industry trends to create a list of prospective growth prospects.

•Be willing to dream large and outside the box.

•Involve your team in the brainstorming process to obtain a variety of viewpoints.

4. Evaluate and prioritize growth opportunities:

•Assess the viability of each development possibility.

•profitability, as well as connection with your entire business objectives.

•Rank growth prospects based on their potential effect and your available resources.

•Create business strategy for each key growth opportunity.

5. Develop and implement growth strategies:

•Develop and execute a clear plan for each growth strategy.

•Assign the resources required to support your growth ambitions.

•Keep track of your progress and make changes as appropriate.

Remember that discovering chances for progress is a constant effort. You may uncover new chances for development and keep ahead of the competition by frequently analyzing your business, target market, and industry trends.

Here are some more ideas for spotting chances for growth:

•Encourage employee feedback: Encourage your staff to share their growth ideas and suggestions. They could have useful insights that you haven't thought about.

•Network with other businesses: Attend industry events and conferences to meet new people and learn about new trends and possibilities.

•Seek expert help: Consider hiring a business consultant or adviser to assist you in identifying and evaluating development prospects.

You may improve your odds of recognizing and pursuing profitable growth opportunities by following these guidelines.

EXPANDING YOUR PRODUCT OR SERVICE AVAILABILITY

Extending your product or service offerings may help your business develop, boost income, and better fulfill the demands of your consumers. However, before growing, you should thoroughly analyze your choices and build a strategic strategy.

Here are some easy ways to broaden your product or service offerings:

•Determine the demands of the customer: What are your consumers requesting? What goods or services do they wish you provided? Conduct market research and surveys to better understand the requirements and desires of your customers.

•Study your competitors: What services or goods do your rivals provide? How can you set yourself apart and provide a superior product?

•Think about your resources: Extending your product or service offerings necessitates the expenditure of resources such as time, money, and experience. Do you have the required resources to enable a successful expansion?

•Create a plan: Once you've discovered prospects for growth, create a thorough strategy. Your objectives, timetable, budget, and marketing plan should all be included.

Here are some particular ways for increasing the number of products or services you offer:

•Introduce new products or services: The most popular approach to extend your product or service offerings is to introduce new products or services. However, it is critical to select goods or services that compliment your present offers and can be supported with your current resources.

•Expand into new markets: Think about entering new geographic areas or focusing on new consumer categories. For example, if you offer things online, you might want to think about expanding into retail storefronts. Alternatively, if you are targeting consumers, you may consider targeting companies.

•Add new features or advantages to your existing offerings: You may also extend your product or service offerings by adding new features or perks to your existing offers. For instance, if you sell software, you may add additional features or capabilities. Alternatively, if you provide a service, you might broaden your service offers to include more services.

•Bundle your products or services: Bundling your present offers is another option to extend your product or service offerings. For example, if you sell software and a training program, you may combine the two and provide a discount to consumers who buy both.

Whatever technique you pick, it is critical to successfully market your increased product or service offerings. Inform your current clients about your new offers and how they will profit from them. You might also need to reach out to new clients to spread the word about your expanding products.

You may effectively extend your product or service options and develop your business by following these guidelines.

GO AFTER A NEW MARKET

A new market might aid in the growth of your business, draw in more customers, and increase revenue. However, you should carefully consider your options and develop a strategic plan before entering a new market.

Here are a few quick tips for entering a new market:

• Choose the right market: Not every market is made equal. To identify markets that are a good fit for your goods or services, conduct market research. Take into account the competitive landscape, market size, and growth potential.

•Construct a market entrance strategy: After deciding on the right market, build a comprehensive plan for entering it. Included should be your marketing plan, budget, schedule, and objectives.

•Create a local presence: In certain situations, creating a local presence in the new market could be advantageous. This might entail opening a physical location, hiring local staff, or working with regional businesses.

•Market your goods or services: After you've made a name for yourself in a new market, you need to draw in potential customers by advertising your goods or services. Make use of a variety of online, offline, and public relations marketing channels.

Here are some specific strategies for entering a new market:

•Collaborate with a nearby company: Collaborating with a nearby company might be an excellent way to easily and quickly enter a new market. The local company can help you connect with potential customers and provide you with helpful market data.

•Going to industry gatherings is a great way to meet potential partners and customers in the new market. It's also a great way to identify patterns and find out more about the market.

•Construct and implement a tailored marketing campaign: Make a campaign that is tailored to the new market. One way to do this may be to integrate regional dialect and customs in your marketing collateral.

• Provide localized pricing: You should think about providing localized pricing to increase the accessibility of your goods or services for customers in the new market.

While breaking into a new market might be challenging, it can also be quite profitable. By implementing these tips, your chances of success could increase.

Here are some additional guidelines for entering a new market:

•Have patience: It takes time to increase sales and brand recognition in a new market. Don't anticipate immediate results.

•Be flexible: Have your strategies ready to adjust as needed. Your strategy might need to change because the new market might not be the same as your current markets.

• Measure your results: Monitor your development and assess the results. This will help you figure out what is and isn't working so you can make the necessary adjustments.

CHAPTER 9 :OVERCOMING OBSTACLES AND MANAGING DIFFICULTIES

Success in many facets of life, including business, requires the capacity to overcome obstacles and manage challenges. For easy reference, use this:

1. Assess the issue or obstacle: The first thing to do is assess the challenge or obstacle that you are facing. What is preventing you from achieving your objective? After identifying the issue, you may begin developing a remedy.

2. Assess the challenge or impediment: After you've identified the obstacle or issue, give it a careful assessment. What fundamental reasons exist? What possible repercussions could arise if the problem is not resolved? What tools and talents do you have to tackle the issue?

3. Formulate a strategy to overcome the obstacle or challenge: Make a plan to get over the difficulty or impediment after evaluating it. A SMART approach (specific, measurable, achievable, relevant, and time-bound) is required for this plan. Additionally, it must be adaptable and adaptive in case circumstances change later.

4. Implement the plan: After you've made a plan, it's time to implement it. It could be necessary to take initiative, assign tasks, and manage

resources. Monitor your development and make adjustments as needed.

5. Take the time to learn from your experiences: Regardless of whether you are able to overcome the obstacle or difficulty, make sure you have learned from it. What worked well? How could you have improved? This knowledge will assist you in better handling obstacles and challenges in the future.

Here are some other suggestions for handling problems and overcoming barriers:

• Remain upbeat and driven: It's important to maintain these traits when faced with obstacles and hurdles. Recall that challenges are something that everyone faces and can overcome.

•Have perseverance: Never give up easily. Keep working on it until you figure something out.

•Ask for help and support: Never be afraid to ask for help and support from other people. There could be others who have gone through comparable struggles and can offer valuable guidance and support.

Recall that overcoming obstacles and overcoming challenges is a normal part of life. By implementing these tips, your chances of success could increase.

OVERCOMING DISASTERS AND FAILURES

There will always be setbacks in life. At some point in their life, everyone experiences them. Knowing how to handle them in a healthy way is essential.

Here are a few guidelines:

• Permit yourself to feel what you're feeling. It's common to feel unhappy, irate, or even angry following a failure or setback. Don't attempt to pretend you're not sad or try to hide your sentiments.

• Ascertain the lessons learned. Every bump and setback presents an opportunity for growth and learning. Give it some thought as to what went wrong and how you might improve moving forward.

• Do not linger on the past. It's important to grow from your mistakes, but you shouldn't dwell on them. Focus on the here and now and the steps you can take to go forward.

•Avoid evaluating yourself against other people. Everybody is traveling a unique route. Comparing yourself to other people will only exacerbate your feelings.

• Seek assistance from others. Talk to a trusted friend, relative, therapist, or anybody else about how you're feeling. You can better control and move on from your emotions by talking about them.

Here are some other coping mechanisms for setbacks and losses:

•Remember that you are not by yourself. Everyone has disappointments and setbacks. Some people have experienced what you are experiencing and come out stronger.

•Never surrender on your goals. It does not follow that you cannot accomplish your goals just because you have a setback or fail. Keep up the fine effort and never give up on your ambitions.

• Take pride in your achievements. Little triumphs ought to be celebrated. You may stay upbeat and motivated by taking the time to recognize and celebrate your successes.

Recall that failures and setbacks are a part of life. You may go forward on your path and cope with them in a healthy way by heeding these tips.

EVALUATING EVOLVING MARKET SITUATIONS

In order to secure sustained success over the long haul, companies of all sizes need to adjust to shifting market dynamics.

Here are some guidelines:

• Recognize market trends: To identify potential shifts and opportunities, monitor market trends and developments. This includes monitoring economic statistics, consumer behavior, and competitive activity.

•Be adaptive and flexible: Be willing to change your business plans and operations in response to changing market conditions. This might include creating new products or services, entering new markets, or modifying your pricing approach.

•Embrace innovation: Adapting to changing market conditions requires embracing innovation. To increase your efficiency and effectiveness, consider new technology, business models, and methods of doing things.

•Invest in your people: Your most valuable asset is your workforce. Invest in their education and training to ensure they have the skills and expertise to assist you in adapting to changing market conditions.

•Inform your clients: Keep your customers up to date on your plans and how you are reacting to changing market conditions. This will aid in retaining their trust and loyalty.

Here are some more pointers for adjusting to shifting market conditions:

•Create a culture of change: Encourage your staff to be open to new ideas and to be open to change. This will enable your company to respond more quickly to shifting market conditions.

•Drive decision-making with data: Use data and analytics to inform your decision-making process. This will assist you in making more informed judgments about how to react to shifting market conditions.

•Be proactive: Do not wait for changes to occur before beginning to adapt. Be proactive in identifying prospective changes so that you can prepare a plan to address them.

Adapting to changing market conditions can be tough, but it is important for all companies. You may improve your chances of success by following these ideas.

Here are some instances of how companies have responded to shifting market conditions:

•Netflix: In response to shifting market conditions, Netflix transitioned from a

DVD-by-mail service to a streaming service. This enabled them to fulfill changing client expectations while remaining competitive in the face of new competition.

•Amazon: Amazon is always inventing and responding to market conditions that change. For example, they created Amazon Web Services (AWS) to provide businesses with cloud computing services. This was done in response to increased demand for cloud computing services.

•Apple: Another corporation noted for its inventiveness and versatility is Apple. For example, to address the increased demand for cell phones, they produced the iPhone. They also launched the iPad, ushering in a new category of electronics.

These are just a few instances of how companies have responded to shifting market conditions. You may boost your chances of success in the ever-changing business market by following their lead.

TAKE DIFFICULT DECISIONS

Making tough choices is a part of life. Everyone has to make them at some time in their lives.

Here are some easy tips for making tough decisions:

•Collect as much information as possible. You will be better able to make a choice if you have more information. Before making a choice, acquire as much information as possible.

•Determine your choices. Determine your choices once you've gathered all of the facts you can. What are all of the choices open to you?

•Weigh the benefits and drawbacks of each choice. Once you've found your alternatives, measure the benefits and drawbacks of each. Consider the likely good and negative repercussions of each choice.

•Observe your gut feelings. Sometimes the best option will be revealed to you by your instincts. When your intuition tells you something different from what your head is telling you, trust it.

• Choose a direction and stay with it. Once you've decided, don't stray from it. Don't think about the possibilities or second-guess yourself. After making your decision, go on.

Here are a few additional guidelines for making challenging choices:

•Never hesitate to ask for help. If you can't decide what to do, talk to a friend, family member, therapist, or anybody else you trust. They are able to provide you guidance and support.

•Take your time. Don't feel pressured to decide right away. Take your time obtaining information, considering your options, and following your instincts.

• Have faith in oneself. You are the most qualified person to make life decisions. Make judgments based on your gut feeling and trust your instincts.

Keep in mind that there is no right or wrong answer when it comes to making tough decisions. Making a decision and moving forward are the most important things. Don't dwell on the possibilities. Simply consider the here and now.

CHAPTER 10: THE ENTREPRENEURIAL JOURNEY : CONCLUSION AND REFLECTIONS

Being an entrepreneur is demanding and satisfying. It is a voyage of learning, growth, and self-discovery. It's a journey full of highs and lows, successes and disappointments.

Here are a few thoughts about the entrepreneurial journey:

•It is a self-discovery adventure. You will discover more about yourself as an entrepreneur than you ever imagined. You will discover your skills and weaknesses, as well as your hobbies and drives. You will also discover how to conquer your anxieties and obstacles.

•It is a learning experience. You will be continually learning as an entrepreneur. You will gain knowledge about your industry, consumers, and competition. You will also gain knowledge in business, marketing, and finance.

•It is a learning experience. As an entrepreneur, you will develop both personally and professionally. You will get new abilities and expertise. You will also gain confidence and resilience.

•The experience is a roller ride. Being a business is not always an easy road. There will be moments in your life when you win and times when you fail. It is crucial to keep in mind that failure is an important component of the learning process. Keep following your goals in spite of setbacks.

•The journey is fraught with ups and downs.Every entrepreneur has both accomplishments and faults. What is important is that you learn from your errors and keep pushing ahead. Don't allow your shortcomings define you.

Here are some recommendations to help you succeed on your job journey:

•Develop a clear objective and purpose statement. What are you attempting to achieve with your company? What is your motivation?

Having a clear vision and objective might aid you in keeping focused and motivated during your trip.

•Be enthused about your company. It would be challenging to attain if you are not passionate about your career. Make sure you're doing something you like and are excited about.

•Be stubborn and strong. The route to business is not always simple. Along the journey, there will be challenges and setbacks. To succeed, it is vital to be persistent and resilient.

•Form a solid team. No business can prosper on his or her own. Surround yourself with people who are talented and tolerant of your views.

•Give something back to your town. Give back to the community that supported you along the way once you've gained success. There are various approaches to do this, including mentoring other entrepreneurs, giving to charity, and providing your time.

The entrepreneurial route is rewarding. You can improve your chances of success by following these ideas.

LESSONS LEARNED FROM THE ENTREPRENEURIAL JOURNEY

Here are some takeaways from the entrepreneurial journey:

•Failure is OK. In reality, failure is an essential component of the learning process. Don't be scared to fail; instead, learn from your errors and keep going.

•Pay attention to your consumers. People will pay you if you solve a real problem for them. Fall in love with your consumers rather than your product or service.

• make a great platoon. You aren't suitable to do everything on your own. Be in the company of others who partake of your enthusiasm and capability for your idea.

• Be patient. Being a business isn't an easy road. You'll ultimately achieve your pretensions if you persist through the ups and campo.

•Enjoy your time! Being an entrepreneur ought to befun.However, it's not worth it, If you are not enjoying yourself.

Here are some more takeaways from the entrepreneurial journey:

•Be prepared to put in long hours. In entrepreneurship, there is no such thing as a get-rich-quick plan. To achieve, you must put in the effort, devotion, and perseverance.

• Do not be spooked to change your mind. Do not be reluctant to modify anything that is not performing. Because the commercial world is continuously evolving, you must be protean.

• Rejoice in your accomplishments. It's critical to fete and appreciate your accomplishments, no matter how minor they may appear. This will help you in remaining motivated and concentrated on your objects.

•Be a part of the entrepreneurial community. Give back to the community that supported you along the path once you've reached success. There are several methods to accomplish this, including mentoring other entrepreneurs, investing in businesses, and contributing to charity.

The entrepreneurial path is lucrative, but it is not for everyone. To achieve, you must put in the effort, devotion, and perseverance. However, if you put in the effort, it may be one of the most gratifying experiences of your life.

TIPS FOR FUTURE ENTREPRENEURS

Here are some pointers for aspiring business owners:

•Look for an issue to fix. The most successful businesses are founded on solving real-world issues for people. Look for a problem in which you have some knowledge and are enthusiastic about tackling.

•Do your homework. It is critical to conduct research before launching your business.

Understanding your target market, rivals, and the industry you're entering are all part of this.

• Construct a business strategy. A business plan is a road map for your organization. It'll help you in defining your objects, strategy, and fiscal prognostications.

• Form a solid platoon. You can not negotiate everything by yourself. compass yourself with individualities who are talented and passionate about your idea.
• Be tenacious. Entrepreneurship is a trip, not an end point. There may be ups and campo along the path, but if you stick with it, you'll eventually reach your objects.

Here are some more pointers for aspiring business owners:

•Begin small. Don't try to accomplish too much too quickly.Begin with a basic product or service offering and gradually expand as your business grows.

•Be customer-focused. Always keep your consumers and their demands in mind. What issues are you resolving for them? What can you do to ease their burden?

•Be thrifty. Don't waste money on frivolous purchases. Every dollar you spend should go toward expanding your business.

•Have patience. Building a successful business takes time. Don't expect to become a success immediately. Simply continue to work hard and learn from your errors.

Entrepreneurship is not for everyone, but it can be extremely rewarding. If you're enthusiastic about fixing people's problems and are prepared to put in the effort, entrepreneurship may be for you.

Don't be hesitant to seek assistance. Mentors, incubators, and accelerators are among the many options accessible to potential entrepreneurs. Utilize these tools and learn from the experiences of others.

CELEBRATING SUCCESS AND LOOK FORWARD TO THE FUTURE

Successes should be celebrated, no matter how minor they appear. Celebrating your accomplishments keeps you motivated and concentrated on your pretensions. It also allows you to appreciate the trouble you have put in. Then are some ideas for fitting your accomplishments.

• Make time for yourself. Do commodities you like and that makes you happy. This might be anything from going out to eat to going for a walk in the forestland.

• Spend time with your family and musketeers. Partake your accomplishments with those who are important to you. They will be pleased for you and will help you in celebrating.

•Give something back to others. Do something pleasant for someone else, such as volunteering or contributing to a good cause. This is a fantastic way to feel good about yourself while also making a positive influence in the world.

After you've enjoyed your accomplishments, it's time to look ahead. What are your future objectives? What do you hope to accomplish? Make a strategy and begin working toward your objectives.

Then are some pointers for looking ahead

• Develop SMART pretensions. Your objects should be unequivocal, quantifiable, attainable, timely, and applicable.

• Divide your pretensions into a lower way. This will make effects appear less intimidating and more attainable.

•Keep track of your progress. This will allow you to assess how far you've come and where you need to improve.

•Don't be hesitant to change your objectives as needed. Because the world is continuously changing, your objectives may need to shift as well.

You may stay motivated and focused on accomplishing your objectives by enjoying your triumphs and looking forward.

REVIEW PAGE

Dear Reader,

I hope you are doing well as I write this! I would like to request your opinion on my most recent book, "Ignite Your Entrepreneurial Spark." I really value your opinions and views, and I'd be interested in knowing how the book went for you.

Your input, no matter how long or how short, is very appreciated. It not only helps us understand how the book spoke to you, but it also helps us create better content in the future. Did the details prove to be useful to you? Did you find any particular sections particularly noteworthy?

Feel free to share your honest thoughts on any platform of your choice, such as Amazon and Goodreads. Your review can make a significant impact and assist other readers in determining whether or not the book is a good fit for them.

I sincerely appreciate you taking the time to express your opinions. I am grateful for your support and want to hear from you!

Warm regards,

Edward D. Rowland

www.ingramcontent.com/pod-product-compliance
Lightning Source LLC
Chambersburg PA
CBHW072155290526
45794CB00004B/1528